THEMATIC UNIT

Peace

Written by Mary Patricia Candace Martin

Illustrated by Sue Fullam

Teacher Created Materials, Inc.
P.O. Box 1040
Huntington Beach, CA 92647
© *1994 Teacher Created Materials, Inc.*
Made in U.S.A.
ISBN 1-55734-248-2

Table of Contents

Introduction

Peace contains a captivating whole language, thematic unit. Its 80 exciting pages are filled with a wide variety of lesson ideas and reproducible pages designed for use with primary children. At its core are two high-quality children's literature selections, *Peace Begins with You* and "Law of the Great Peace" (found in *The Big Book for Peace*). For each of these books, activities are included which set the stage for reading, encourage the enjoyment of the book, and extend the concepts gained. In addition, the theme is connected to the curriculum with activities in language arts (including daily writing suggestions), math, science, social studies, art, music, and life skills. Many of these activities encourage cooperative learning. Suggestions and patterns for bulletin boards and unit management tools are additional time savers for the busy teacher. Furthermore, directions for student-created Big Books and a culminating activity, both of which allow students to synthesize their knowledge in order to produce products that can be shared beyond the classroom, highlight this very complete teacher resource.

This thematic unit includes:

☐ **literature selections** — summaries of two children's books with related lessons (complete with reproducible pages) that cross the curriculum.

☐ **poetry** — suggested selections and lessons enabling students to write and publish their own works.

☐ **planning guides** — suggestions for sequencing lessons each day of the unit.

☐ **writing ideas** — daily suggestions as well as writing activities across the curriculum.

☐ **bulletin board ideas** — suggestions and plans for student-created and/or interactive bulletin boards.

☐ **homework suggestions** — extending the unit to the child's home.

☐ **curriculum connections** — in language arts, math, science, social studies, art, music, and life skills.

☐ **group projects** — to foster cooperative learning.

☐ **culminating activity** — which requires students to synthesize their learning to produce a product or engage in an activity that can be shared with others.

☐ **bibliography** — suggesting additional literature and nonfiction books on the theme.

To keep this valuable resource intact so that it can be used year after year, you may wish to punch holes in the pages and store them in a three-ring binder.

Introduction *(cont.)*

Why Whole Language?

A whole language approach involves children in using all modes of communication: reading, writing, listening, observing, illustrating, experiencing, and doing. Communication skills are interconnected and integrated into lessons that emphasize the whole of language rather than isolating its parts. The lessons revolve around selected literature. Reading is not taught as a separate subject from writing and spelling, for example. A child reads, writes (spelling appropriately for his/her level), speaks, listens, etc. in response to a literature experience introduced by the teacher. In this way, language skills grow naturally, stimulated by involvement and interest in the topic at hand.

Why Thematic Planning?

One very useful tool for implementing an integrated whole language program is thematic planning. By choosing a theme with correlative literature selections for a unit of study, a teacher can plan activities throughout the day that lead to a cohesive, in-depth study of the topic. Students will be practicing and applying their skills in meaningful contexts. Consequently, they will tend to learn and retain more. Both teachers and students will be freed from a day that is broken into unrelated segments of isolated drill and practice.

Why Cooperative Learning?

Besides learning academic skills and content, students need to learn social skills. No longer can this area of development be taken for granted. Students must learn to work cooperatively in groups in order to function well in modern society. Group activities should be a regular part of school life and teachers should consciously include social objectives as well as academic objectives in their planning. For example, a group working together to write a report may need to select a leader. The teacher should make clear to the students and monitor the qualities of good leader-follower group interaction just as he/she would state and monitor the academic goals of the project.

Why Big Books?

An excellent cooperative, whole language activity is the production of Big Books. Groups of students, or the whole class, can apply language skills, content knowledge, and creativity to produce a Big Book that can become a part of the classroom library to be read and reread. These books make excellent culminating projects for sharing beyond the classroom with parents, librarians, other classes, etc. Big Books can be reproduced in many ways and this thematic unit book includes directions for at least one method you may choose.

Peace Begins with You

by Katherine Scholes

Summary

This book begins with personal needs and wants. It then increases the scope beyond the individual to include the appreciation of diversity, such as living alone versus living with others. It also names skills needed in living peacefully — listening to each other, problem-solving, cooperating, mediating problems, alternative-setting, and decision-making. The book then moves into a discussion of conflict as a possible beginning of understanding. Nations and groups can also find themselves in need of mediation. Peacemakers are mentioned as hard workers because peacemaking is much harder than fighting.

This is a book children enjoy, but they do need teacher assistance to pull apart and examine the different aspects of peace that are available to them, and to practice those skills.

Sample Plan

Day I

- Do Peace and Nature. (page 8)
- Begin reading *Peace Begins with You.*

Day II

- Finish *Peace Begins with You.*
- Put up Bulletin Board. Use daily for opening.
- Share peaceful music. (pages 13-14)
- Build a Peaceful Construction. (pages 43-44)
- Make Peace Journal entry. (page 33)
- Make Mandalas. (page 65)
- Construct the Validation Station. (pages 25-27)

Day III

- Continue bulletin board opening.
- Explain validation station; write two validations.
- Share several peaceful "cuts" from audiotapes.
- Role play peace roles. (page 9)
- Record results on writing activity.
- Make a Human Pretzel. (page 37)
- Make Peace Journal entry. (page 34)

Day IV

- Continue bulletin board opening.
- Write three validations.
- Share several peaceful selections.
- Conduct a peace interview. (page 15)
- Have students begin to collect peace and war newspaper/magazine articles. (page 47)
- Make My Pyramid of Peace. (page 11)

Day V

- Continue bulletin board opening.
- Write two validations.
- Share peaceful musical selections.
- Brainstorm for Peace Web. (page 10)
- Continue Peace/War articles chart follow-up in daily writing.
- Make Peace Doves and display. (page 74)
- Write a sequel to *Peace Begins with You.* (page 16)
- Review friendly letters. Write to peacemakers. (page 17)

Overview of Activities

SETTING THE STAGE

1. Begin the bulletin board. See pages 72-73. Use it as an opening to your day's lessons.

2. Do "Peace and Nature" (page 8) before reading *Peace Begins with You* or *The Big Book for Peace*. Save these papers. After finishing the unit, ask children to reevaluate their answers. Does peace mean the same thing to all of them?

3. Put the Peace Journal together. See directions on page 33. This may be done as a whole group project. Make sure to add blank paper for children to record their thoughts throughout the unit.

4. Decorate the envelopes that will be used for the Validation Station. Provide one envelope per child. Make sure that children put their first names on their envelopes. See page 25.

5. Prepare paper for mandala art. See page 65.

6. Reproduce peace doves on page 74 for students. Use these doves in a variety of ways. Prepare them for peaceful acts that students observe others doing, as well as to describe their own peaceful acts. Use them in your classroom to help decorate and reinforce the peace theme.

ENJOYING THE BOOK

1. Show the students the cover of *Peace Begins with You* and ask for their thoughts. Ask them how peace begins with them. Place their thoughts on a chart and save. You will add to the chart throughout the week.

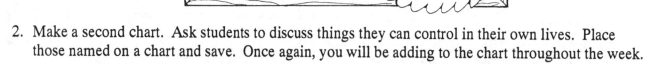

2. Make a second chart. Ask students to discuss things they can control in their own lives. Place those named on a chart and save. Once again, you will be adding to the chart throughout the week.

3. Begin by reading the book straight through. Let the children listen and enjoy the story.

4. After you have read the story through, follow the procedure outlined below. This will give the children time to reflect on the book.

   • Begin by reading again, this time stopping after "...having the things you need." Ask students to name some things they need. Read on until "...at least some of the things you want." Stop there and ask students to name some things they want, but that they could live without.

   • Read on until "...allowed to be different." Ask students to tell you how being allowed to be different happens. How do people know when they are allowed to be different?

　　　　　6

Overview of Activities (cont.)

ENJOYING THE BOOK (cont.)

- Read on until "...conflict as a beginning." Ask how conflict can be the beginning for students when they disagree on the playground.

- Read on until "...choices." Ask how the choices we make can affect those around us.

- Read on until "...peace with the land." Ask students how we do that today, and how we could be even better at it tomorrow. Why is living with the earth so important to all of us?

5. Re-read the book again urging students to think back to the points that they brought up during class discussions. This re-reading opportunity will give students a chance to hear some things they may have missed before.

EXTENDING THE BOOK

---

1. Begin the "Sounds of Peace" song search. See page 13.

2. Begin looking for peace in the news. It would be helpful to demonstrate scanning a newspaper, identifying a peaceful article, cutting it out, and displaying it for the first two days. Then, leave it up to students to do the scan (page 47).

3. Have your students teach another classroom how to make mandalas. Working cooperatively with another class of students their own age will reinforce the importance of cooperative team skill-building.

4. Create an ongoing hallway display of peaceful news articles. Title it "Peace Wall." Challenge other students in the school to find peaceful articles to add to the "Peace Wall."

5. Begin a research project (page 60). Use famous peacemakers as the springboard for research. Let students work with a partner.

6. Make Peacemaker Trading Cards. See directions and format on page 56. Have children extend the activity by making their own cards using the blank card provided.

7. Share the trading cards with younger "book buddies." Have your students encourage their buddies to read about the peacemaker on the trading card. Encourage the children in your class to trade the cards among themselves.

8. Do the Pyramid of Peace (page 11) with the children. Before doing this, review the words that represent the group interdependence. Explain what each one is and have the children rank them from the smallest to the largest. These will be: you, family, neighborhood, community, state or province, nation, continent, world.

Name _____

Peace and Nature

In the book *Peace Begins with You* there is this message:

"But all living things are part of one giant web of life.
And — in the end — they all depend on one another.
So when we think about the future,
We must think about living in peace with the land."

What do these words mean to you? Write your feelings here.

_____

_____

_____

_____

_____

In *The Big Book for Peace* there is the "Law of the Great Peace," part of which states:

"Roots have spread out from the Tree of Great Peace one to the north, one to the east, one to the south, and one to the west. These are the Great White Roots, and their nature is peace and strength."

How did the Iroquois Law demonstrate the Iroquois way of living in peace with the land? Write those ways here.

_____

_____

_____

_____

_____

8

Peace Roles

Often we find ourselves in non-peaceful situations. If we have discussed them in advance, we can sometimes remember alternatives or other ways of doing things. Explain this to the children. Tell them that this is what they are about to do now.

Choose one or more people to do the role play. You may wish to let the children choose their own partners or groups. Discuss who is who, and what each role will include.

First, do a role play with a non-peaceful result. Discuss with the class what has happened. Then have children do the same role-play but with peaceful results. Discuss with the class what occurred the second time.

Ask the whole group which was the most respectful way to handle the situation. Discuss the meaning of respect.

Below are just a few ideas for role plays to get you started. You and your class will certainly have others to add.

Ideas for Role Playing

- At recess, three people want to play with one ball.

- At lunch, two people want to sit in the same spot.

- In the classroom, someone takes your pencil.

- At recess, two people continually interrupt your game.

- In the hallway, two people are pushing in the water fountain line.

- In the bathroom, you see someone pull all of the remaining paper towels out of the dispenser and place them in the sink.

- You are in line for the drinking fountain, and a student cuts in front of you.

- A student in class keeps calling out while the teacher is reading a story to the class.

Peace Web

Adjectives are descriptive words. For example, look at the following sentence:

> The *warm* sun beat down on the *happy* children as they played together.

The word *warm* is an adjective describing the sun, and the word *happy* describes the children.

Read through *Peace Begins with You* and find adjectives that describe what peace is. Write some of them here.

_____ _____ _____ _____

Now, using the adjectives, create a web with the word "peace" in the middle.

Challenge: Number the adjectives in the order they are used in the story. Draw a picture for each.

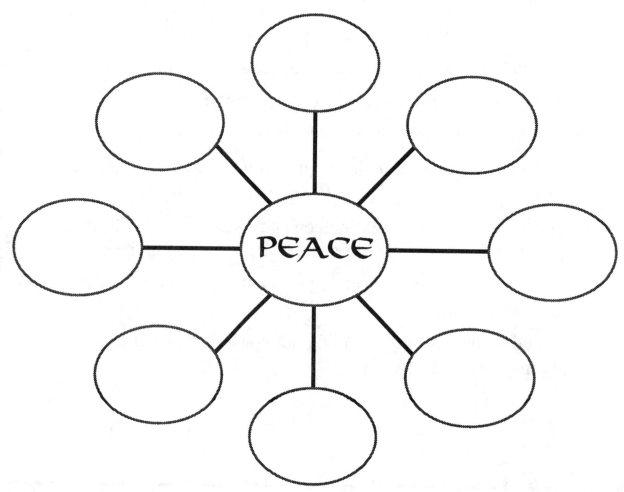

10   ©1994 *Teacher Created Materials, Inc.*

My Pyramid of Peace

This is called an inverted (upside down) pyramid. It will help you see how we are all interdependent on (need) each other. It gets larger and larger as you move from the point at the bottom.

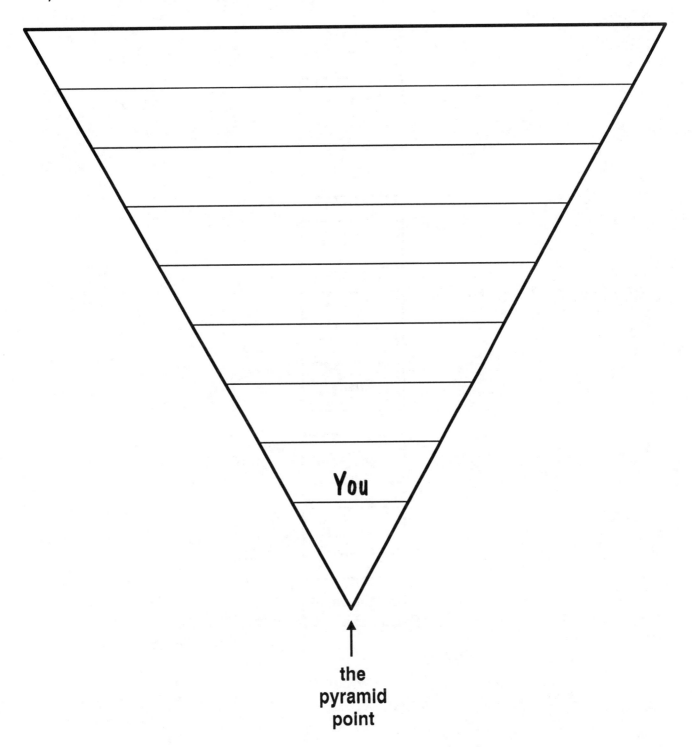

You

↑
the
pyramid
point

My Pyramid of Peace (cont.)

Directions: Cut out the words below. Put them in order from the smallest to the largest group. Glue them onto the pyramid on page 11, from the smallest on the bottom, to the largest on the top. You may color your pyramid or draw pictures.

Community

World

Continent

State or Province

Family

Nation

You

Neighborhood

12

The Sounds of Peace

Peace Begins with You stresses that "peace is something that lives, grows, spreads — and needs to be looked after."

Try these two activities as you listen to the sounds of peace. One you will do at school. One you will do at home and share with your classmates.

At School

You will need a battery-powered tape recorder and a blank audio cassette. At recess, take the tape outside with you. Push the record button. Tape the sounds you hear. These might include your friends at play on the playground, birds singing, or any sounds of nature you can hear outside. Play the tape at school.

What does peace sound like? Draw a picture or write in the space below.

The Sounds of Peace *(cont.)*

At Home

Music is very important in our world. It can soothe us after a tiring day, energize us when we are feeling low, make us laugh, or teach us through a song's lyrics.

Listen to some of your favorite music at home. These can be records, tapes, CDs, written words to which you know the melody, or songs on the radio. Play them, or sing them at home for practice. Then record or learn the part of the song that is peaceful to you. Take it to school and play or sing it for your classmates. Tell why you think it is peaceful. Recognize that peace sounds differently to different people.

With your teacher, create a chart of the chosen songs. List the name of the song and the reason it was chosen on the chart.

Name of Song	Reason Chosen
_____	_____
_____	_____
_____	_____
_____	_____
_____	_____
_____	_____
_____	_____
_____	_____
_____	_____
_____	_____
_____	_____

Peace Interview

Interview three of your friends on the playground. Ask each friend a different question from below. Record the person's first name and his or her answer. The questions are about possible incidents.

Incident #1

Name _____

What would you do if someone took the ball you and your friend were playing with?

_____

_____

Incident #2

Name _____

What would you do if you saw your friend being teased and called names on the playground?

_____

_____

Incident #3

Name _____

What would you do if someone pushed into you repeatedly during recess?

_____

_____

Now, look at the three interviews. Can you think of another way to handle each? Write down the alternative way; make sure it is different.

Incident #1 - _____

Incident #2 - _____

Incident #3 - _____

Can there be two ways to handle the same incident? Yes/No.

What do differences help us to realize about our friends?

You Are a Peacemaker

You are the main character in the book, *Peace Begins with You*. What happens next? Write a sequel. A sequel is the story of what comes next after the book ends. Begin your sequel at the end of the book.

Before writing the sequel, think about these questions:

How do you become a peacemaker?

What steps do you go through to create peace in your own neighborhood? In your own school? In your own family?

How would you change the non-peaceful area of your life?

Now you are the author. Write your story here.

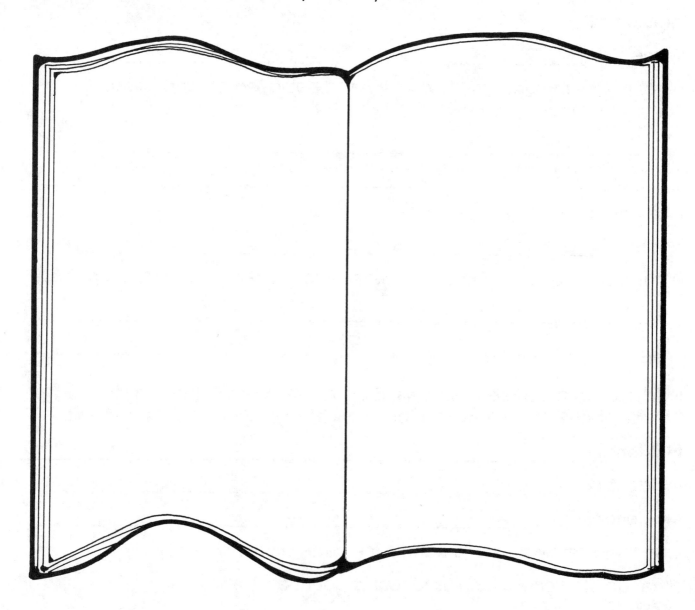

Letter Writing

Peace Begins with You encourages the readers to find out what is happening in the world around them. A good way to do this is to write letters. Review the friendly letter format below.

Friendly Letter

Heading (Address)   Date

Salutation (Starts with "Dear...")

Body (Information)

_____

_____

_____

Closing (Ending word or words)

Signature (Letter writer's name, printed or signed)

Then have students write letters to world leaders whose countries are in conflict. They may wish to use the stationery on page 78. In their letters have them include these questions:

- What does peace mean to you?
- Why is it important?
- Who are you?
- How can a leader have peace?
- Where do you live?
- What are some of your ideas on how to settle the conflict in your country?

Remember to include your school address, just in case a response is written!

"Law of the Great Peace"

from *The Big Book for Peace*

adapted by John Bierhorst

from the Iroquois Book of the Great Law

"Law of the Great Peace" is an adaptation of the Iroquois Book of the Great Law. *Deganawida founded the League of Five Nations composed of the Mohawk, Oneida, Onondaga, Cayuga, and Seneca nations. Told with nature as the example, it presents the way that the five member nations shall conduct their actions. It stresses the importance of hospitality, communication, listening, and fair decision-making. It also makes clear that the five nations must remain accessible to those in need and to those who desire a peace agreement with the five nations.*

Sample Plan

Day I

- Create a bulletin board opening. (pages 72-73)
- Begin each day by saying peace in a different language. (page 53)
- Demonstrate how to scan peace articles.
- Read "Law of the Great Peace."
- Do Peace Wheels as follow-up to reading.
- Have students begin to search through their personal audio cassette collections for peaceful music. Have them share.

Day II

- Continue bulletin board opening.
- Draw the Tree of Peace. (page 21)
- Write three validations. (page 26)
- Do Broken Squares activity. (pages 38-42)
- Write an entry in Peace Journals. (page 33)
- Begin Research Project. (page 60)

Day III

- Continue bulletin board opening.
- Write three validations.
- Share musical selections.
- Continue Research Project.

Day IV

- Continue bulletin board opening.
- Write two validations.
- Share peaceful music record results.
- Rehearse Peace Roles with partners. Act them out for the class. (page 9)
- Hold a Peace Fair. (pages 28-29)
- Continue Research project. (This may become homework.)

Day V

- Continue bulletin board opening.
- Finish Research Project.
- Write two validations.
- Share musical selections
- Discuss Peace Pole as culminating activity and develop a plan. (page 68)

Day VI

- Continue bulletin board opening.
- Write two validations.
- Examine news/magazine articles. (page 47)
- Make Peace Quilt. (pages 70-71)

Overview of Activities

SETTING THE STAGE

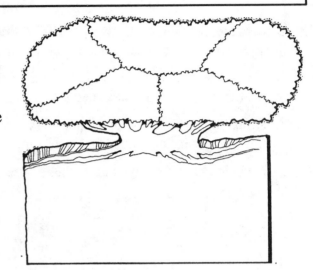

1. Complete "Harmony with Others" drawing before you read. Ask students to draw their own idea of a peaceful tree, adding friends and family beneath the branches (page 24).

2. Discuss the connection between people and nature in Native American life. Ask for examples of similar connections in students' lives. (Pets are terrific examples).

3. Turn students' attention to the bulletin board that has begun reflecting student and societal attitudes and visions of peace. (Discuss any thoughts that come from focusing upon it.)

4. Remind students that they will be searching through their own cassette collection to find peaceful selections that they would like to bring to class to share (page 14).

5. Remind students that you or they have already read the book, *Peace Begins with You*. The discussion that followed that book also has helped to set the scene for this one.

6. Play any Native American music you may have — the more peaceful, the better, to further set the stage.

7. Read the "Law of the Great Peace" all the way through first. Discuss after you have finished.

ENJOYING THE BOOK

1. Before reading, ask the students to tell you what is needed to solve a problem between two or more people. List the things that they name. Then, have three strips ready. Label the strips:

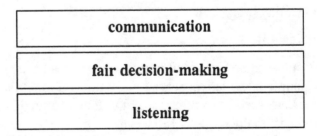

communication
fair decision-making
listening

Have students tape each strip to the board. Cut the list into strips (one idea per strip). Have the students help you organize the ideas they had named under the appropriate headings.

2. Teacher note: Read the background information about the League first. Share the background information with the children. This would be best done in a storytelling mode to engage and intrigue the students.

Overview of Activities

ENJOYING THE BOOK (cont.)

---

3. Discuss the meaning of the word "alien" in the story. An alien is a person from a country other than your own. In this case, it is not about creatures from other planets.

4. Ask the students to close their eyes as you read. Encourage them to imagine themselves in the story of the "Law of the Great Peace."

5. After reading, ask them to open their eyes. Discuss what they were — were they the tree? a brave warrior? an observing animal? a chief? a member of an alien nation seeking help from the League?

6. As a whole group activity, create a huge "tree of peace" mural.

Ask students how they will show that a welcome is ready to those who need to be added later, or to those who need help.

EXTENDING THE BOOK

---

1. Draw the Tree of Peace meeting (page 21).

2. Do the "Peace Wheel" (page 46).

3. Use the "Validation Station" as an extension of both books (pages 25-27). For one week, write encouragement notes to people who were observed working well together. Another week, the focus could be on being a kind friend. Another week the focus could be on responsibility. Some week's validations may be left to the focus of the writer.

4. Do "The Human Pretzel" activity to demonstrate (physically) the need for cooperation in problem-solving (page 37).

5. Use some of the other stories in *The Big Book for Peace*. Choose from the ideas on page 32.

6. Involve children in "Playground Conflict . . . Peaceful Solutions" (page 48) as a way to show how math and peace interact.

The Tree of Peace

Deganawida planted the tree of peace and founded the League of Five Nations uniting the Mohawk, Oneida, Onondaga, Cayuga, and the Seneca Peoples.

Draw the meeting of the League beneath the tree.

Seneca

Oneida

Cayuga

Onondaga

Mohawk

The Tree of Peace (cont.)

Why do you think the tree was used as the symbol of peace by Deganawida?

_____

_____

_____

_____

_____

_____

_____

_____

_____

Cut out these labels and glue them to the parts of the tree they represent:

| foundation of peace | growth of peace | spreading of peace |

Harmony with Nature

Native Americans live in harmony with nature. How can you and your friends also live in harmony with nature? List what you can do to live peacefully with animals and the land. Write your ideas here.

We can live in harmony by:

1. _____

_____

_____

2. _____

_____

_____

3. _____

_____

_____

4. _____

_____

_____

5. _____

_____

_____

6. _____

_____

_____

Harmony with Others

What is a Tree of Peace? What do you think it looks like? Draw your own Tree of Peace. Make it as beautiful as possible. Add your friends and family beneath its branches.

Validation Station

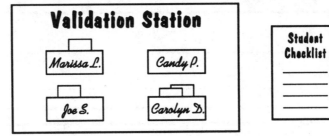

Creating a classroom Validation Station creates a positive classroom climate and also gives a meaningful reason to write. Validations are specific, positive messages written to members of the class. They are written during "Validation Time." It is important that the teacher writes validations along with the students and delivers them — students really look forward to these positive comments!

Follow the directions below and construct a classroom Validation Station.

Materials: Small envelopes for each student (often card
and gift shops will share their unused envelopes)

Crayons or colored pencils

Student checklist for each student (page 27)

Validation cards (page 26)

Posterboard (enough to accommodate envelopes for your class)

Strapping tape or rubber cement

How To Make the Validation Station

- Prepare envelopes by cutting off the sticky flap. Have each student place his or her first name and last initial on the flap-side of the envelope and decorate colorfully. Tape or glue envelopes onto the posterboard. Don't forget an envelope for the teacher, too!

- Post a checklist with all the students' names on it next to the Validation Board. As students put a validation into an envelope, it should be checked off.

How To Use the Validation Station

Validation language must be used as the beginning of the specific positive comment. The validation cards on page 26 may be used or students may use them as sentence starters. As soon as one person has been validated, the student-writer dates the validated person's name on the checklist. Student-writers then "deliver" the validations to the student envelope in the validation station. Validation stations are emptied once per week. Validations are then read and taken home.

Post the validation cards in the validation station. These eight sentence starters are the only way that validations may begin. Therefore, the message is positive each and every time validations are written. Discuss the importance of specifics — that is, to write "I like you" may be nice, but a more specific message would be "I like the way you helped me at lunch today! Thanks!" The more specific the message the more sincere the message is to the reader. Practice along with students for the first few weeks. Teachers need to write the messages, also.

Validation Language

I admire _____
_____

I applaud _____
_____

I appreciate _____
_____

I celebrate _____
_____

I cherish _____
_____

I like _____
_____

I love _____
_____

I compliment _____
_____

26

Student Checklist for Validation

Student Name	Date of Validation
1.	
2.	
3.	
4.	
5.	
6.	
7.	
8.	
9.	
10.	
11.	
12.	
13.	
14.	
15.	
16.	
17.	
18.	
19.	
20.	
21.	
22.	
23.	
24.	
25.	
26.	
27.	
28.	
29.	
30.	

Peace Fair

After finishing "Law of the Great Peace" hold a class or school-wide peace fair. The peace fair can include:

- **Mural-making** — Provide students with colored paper, tempera paints, and brushes. Attach the colored paper to the floor. Working together, students create three murals. On one they will paint their ideas of peace for their school. On another, they'll paint peace in their city or town and on the last one, peace in the world.

- **Torn Paper Activity** — Cover several large refrigerator boxes with bulletin board paper. Students will make large-sized collages of themselves solving problems at school, home, and/or in their community.

- **War Toys, Peace Toys** — Display a collection of war toys and peace toys. Provide a tape recorder with a blank audio cassette on a table. Encourage students to speak their thoughts on the differences they see between the two kinds of toys. Also ask them if they think the toys that are played with have any effect on the real-life conflicts during recess.

- **Where in the World Is Peace?** — Hang a large world map on one wall. Provide red and blue dots, atlases, and reference books on a table near the map. Encourage students to place red dots for places in current conflict and blue dots where there is no conflict present.

- **What's New?** — Provide copies of current newspapers and glue. Divide a large piece of butcher paper into two large columns labeled "Peace" and "War." Encourage students to cut out articles that they find on both topics and glue them under the appropriate heading.

- **Let's Resolve It!** — Provide copies of current newspapers, glue, pencils, and paper. Label a large piece of butcher paper, "Problems in the News — Let's Resolve Them!" Find problems in the newspaper, and have students write their solutions and glue them side-by-side.

28

Peace Fair *(cont.)*

- **Games Area** — These games may be played:

  Observation Game — You will need several parents or high schoolers to run this game. First, ask participants to find someone in the group who has something like theirs. (Example: Find someone in the group with the same color tennis shoes you are wearing.)

  Then, sit back to back. Now, each of you change three things about your appearance. When everyone is ready, turn, face each other, and taking turns, try to find the three things that were changed! (Example: Push hair behind ear, roll up pants leg, take a sock off.)

  Find a new partner and repeat.

  Human Sculpture Game — Explain to students that they are going to make a machine using their bodies. Begin with two students. Then have five other students, one at a time, come forward and attach themselves to the first two. Then, when all have been added, ask them to begin their lives as one machine and begin to move. Next, have them make the noises that match their actions. Have them freeze and hold their pose. Discuss the need for cooperation to run this machine.

  Rain — This game uses the energies of each member of the group to produce the sound of a thunderstorm. Students sit in a large circle, facing the center, with their eyes closed. They will be told to repeat the sound made by the person to their right. In this way, the sound will travel around the circle. The leader begins by rubbing palms together back and forth, continuing this until the sound has come full circle. When it has come all the way around to the leader's right, the leader begins snapping fingers in the same way.

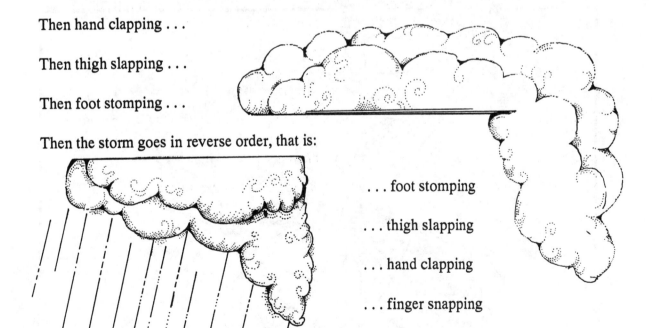

Then hand clapping . . .

Then thigh slapping . . .

Then foot stomping . . .

Then the storm goes in reverse order, that is:

. . . foot stomping

. . . thigh slapping

. . . hand clapping

. . . finger snapping

. . . palm rubbing

. . . then quiet.

Make Your Own Big Book

When students make a Big Book, they recreate the story they have read in a new and different way. They demonstrate their understanding of that story on many levels.

Materials: Paper — 11" x 17" (28 cm x 43 cm)

Markers, crayons, colored pencils

Hole punch

Yarn

Directions: Explain Big Books to children. Decide whether students will create Big Books individually, in a group, or as a class. Since the "Law of the Great Peace" is done in stanzas, each stanza could become a page or more depending on its length.

- The pages could then be put together to form a class Big Book.

- The children can retell the story in their own words to an adult who writes the text at the bottom of the page. Children may also write their own text.

- The pages should then be illustrated by the student authors. Make a cover. Use the pattern on page 31 to help children create a cover. This can be colored, cut out, and glued onto a large sheet of paper. Make sure that all the authors and illustrators are listed on the cover.

- The book can be bound by punching holes and putting yarn through. Share the book with the class. Make sure to include it in the classroom library.

Make Your Own Big Book (cont.)

This is

_____

(class)

Big Book

of

"Law of the Great Peace"

Authors and Illustrators

Extending *The Big Book for Peace*

The "Law of the Great Peace" is found in the *The Big Book for Peace*. This book was created by over 30 children's authors and illustrators. Choose some of the other stories and read them to the class. Read them strictly for enjoyment or try one of the activities listed below.

"The Dream" by Steven Kellogg

Have children describe a dream they might envision about peace. Have them draw pictures that describe their dreams. Display the pictures.

"The Two Brothers" by Lloyd Alexander

Have children make a positive/negative art project. They will need two contrasting colors of construction paper, scissor, glue, and tape. Have them cut each sheet of construction paper in half; tape two opposite colors together and reserve the remaining halves. Place the remaining halves on top of one another and cut out a design. Glue each design piece to its contrasting background.

"The Tree House" by Lois Lowry

Based on the descriptions given in the story, draw and color pictures of Chrissy's and Leah's tree houses. Ask children if they've ever spent time in a tree house.

"The Bus for Deadhorse" by Natalie Babbitt

Divide the children into groups of three or four. Give each group some soda crackers, perforated crackers, a handful of popcorn, etc. Make sure that the amounts given to each group cannot be divided evenly among them. Have the groups divide the food fairly. Discuss how, or if, they were able to resolve any problems.

"The Bird's Peace" by Jean Craighead George

Discuss how Kristy dealt with her fears in the story. Ask the children how they would feel if someone they loved suddenly had to go to war. Who would they talk to? With the class, write a list of ways children can overcome and cope with a fearful situation.

"A Ruckus" by Thacher Hurd

Group the students. Have them create cartoons for their own peaceful ruckus.

My Peace Journal

Create a Peace Journal for each student. The journal will allow the children to reflect on the activities they do during the peace unit and on their own feelings. Pages 34-36 will be needed for each student. Add both lined and unlined paper. Cut the paper to fit the journal so that the lines are available for thoughts and feelings. Let students create a cover using colorful construction paper or the one provided. Encourage them to decorate it with their own symbols of peace and add their name on the cover. The activities that are included in their journals, and a page that can be used first for writing, are found on pages 14, 34, and 37.

Cover of Journal

Name _____

My Peace Journal *(cont.)*

Music of Peace

We were asked to go through our own collections of taped music and to find songs that were peaceful. We brought them in and shared them, along with the reasons they were chosen. I chose:

Song Title _____

Artist Name _____

Reasons for Selection _____

_____

_____

Questions about the sounds of peace in music:

1. Were you ever surprised by a selection? Which one(s)? Why?

2. How can peace sound so different to each person?

3. What is peace?

4. How was your definition of peace changed since hearing different selections of music?

The Human Pretzel

We were asked to have two people leave the room while the rest of us held hands and tangled ourselves up. The two people who left the room came back to untangle us.

Here is a drawing of what we looked like forming the Human Pretzel.

I felt _____

I would like to do it differently next time. Here's what I would change:

_____

34

My Peace Journal *(cont.)*

Broken Squares

As a group we were asked to make five squares of equal size by sharing and trading pieces of the squares.

My group completed the square by _____

_____

_____

This is how our square was put together

Peace in the News

We were asked to begin a collection of newspapers and magazines. We were then asked to find articles on peace.

This article is from the week of _____

Here are headlines of articles:

_____

_____

_____

It is interesting that the newspapers and magazines seem to write (focus) on _____

I think a possible reason for the focus may be _____

If I were a newspaper/magazine journalist, I would _____

My Peace Journal *(cont.)*

My Thoughts About Peace

Peace Construction

We were asked to construct a design using toothpicks and popcorn. First, we did this independently. Then, we linked ours with another design. We found out that interdependence means to rely on each other for support.

Positive things I learned about interdependence

This is what my design looked like.

Some negative things I found about interdependence are

My own thoughts about interdependence are

This is what my design looked like after linking it to others.

Peace Journal Activities

Cooperation — A Skill for Peace

The Human Pretzel

To make a human pretzel follow the directions below.

Two people leave the room. Others hold hands and twist themselves over, under, and through each other without letting go. The two people come back in and untangle the group. The group cooperates as the untanglers direct.

The Pretzel Variation

Everyone in the circle puts out their right hand and takes the right hand of someone else. Then they put out their left hand and take someone's left hand (if an odd number of students, one person waits until second time and puts out both hands). The group then works to untangle itself.

When untangled, some will be facing the opposite direction.

If the group does not disentangle in a few minutes, tell them not to worry; just try again, splitting the group into two smaller circles. If everyone in the whole world did it, they could end up in a perfect circle; you just have to break it down to a manageable size!

Teacher Directions: This experiential game is used to focus on the patience/impatience within the group, the force used among the group, and the cooperative attitude that develops among group members.

Use conflict, if it arises, to demonstrate the need for cooperation when in a group. Discuss what cooperation feels like.

Repeat this exercise several times throughout the unit and you will see improvement as the understanding of the purpose of the game is increased.

Peace Journal Activities *(cont.)*

Broken Squares

Making the Squares

A complete set of squares for the classroom consists of five envelopes. Each envelope contains a piece of cardboard which has been cut into a different pattern and which, when properly assembled, form five squares of equal size. One set is provided for each group.

To make a set, reproduce the patterns on this page and page 39. Mark five envelopes with the letters A, B, C, D, and E. Distribute the puzzle pieces in the envelopes.

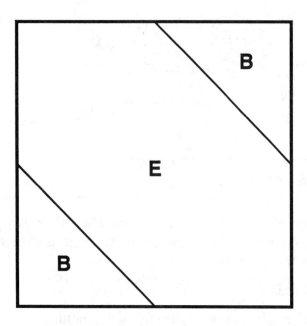

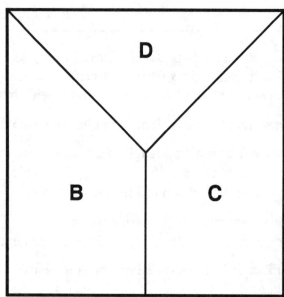

Peace Journal Activities *(cont.)*

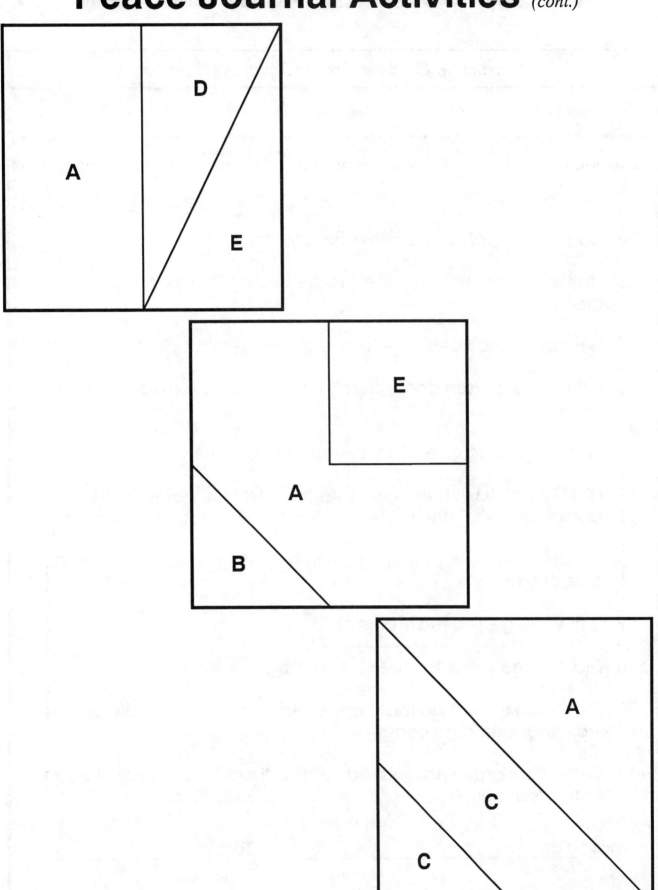

Peace Journal Activities *(cont.)*

Instruction Card for Broken Squares Observer

Reproduce this card for those who will act as observers.

1. No talking, pointing, or any other signaling in the group.

2. No grabbing of pieces from one another.

3. No throwing pieces into the middle of the table for others to grab.

4. Give one piece at a time to one group member directly.

5. If the other person does not take the piece right away, take it back.

6. Who is willing to give away pieces of the puzzle?

7. Did anyone finish his/her own square and then not want to participate with others?

8. Is there anyone who struggles with his/her own pieces, but won't give any away?

9. Is anyone getting really angry?

10. Did anyone break the rules by pointing or talking?

11. Was there something that happened to make the whole group work together all at once?

12. When your group has finished, remind them to sit quietly. Report to the teacher.

Name _____ Date _____

Peace Journal Activities *(cont.)*

Broken Squares Instructions

This simulation reveals aspects of cooperation in solving a group problem. It will show the students their own productive and obstructive behaviors in solving group problems.

Read the following group instructions to the children.

1. You will each be given an envelope with pieces of cardboard for forming squares.

2. At the signal to begin, your group will make five squares of equal size, so that each person has one square in front of him/her, equal in size to the others in the group.

3. You may give away your pieces directly to other participants, and you may receive pieces given directly to you by them. You may even give away all the pieces to your puzzle, even after you have already formed a square.

4. You Must Obey the Following Rules:

   • No talking.

   • No grabbing anyone's puzzle piece.

   • No signaling for a piece.

   • No showing someone where the piece belongs.

   Teacher Note: Check for understanding. Model acceptable squares and unacceptable squares, if necessary.

5. Each group has an official observer.

6. Observers have instruction cards in their hands. (See observer card, page 40.)

7. Observers will read aloud each of the parts of his/her job.

8. Observers will have clipboards to note their observations. Check with observers. Be sure they understand their role. Ask for questions from the groups.

9. Some groups will finish before others. If your group finishes early, sit quietly until the others finish. Do not help anyone who is having difficulty.

10. Listen for the signal to begin.

11. When all groups have finished, open with the observers' reports. Stress the fact that this is what the observer saw as he/she did his/her job.

12. Open the discussion to the entire group — focus on feelings during the simulation. Ask students to compare it to real life. When have you felt that way before? What were you doing? How did you work it out?

Peace Journal Activities *(cont.)*

Broken Squares Discussion

When you have finished the broken squares simulation, hold a discussion. Bring out the following:

- Point out how observing others' needs helps the entire group.

- Point out the need for humans to communicate in order to cooperate. Point out that it does not help others to give them too much help. How is that like school?

- The group was given a task. Almost everyone feels an initial closure when an individual square is completed. Yet that complete square may prevent other people from completing theirs.

How does that relate to tasks given to us in our day-to-day lives? Use the lines below to note the relationship to our lives. Use these as further discussion or writing activities for children.

_____

_____

_____

_____

_____

_____

_____

_____

_____

_____

_____

_____

_____

_____

_____

_____

_____

Peace Journal Activities *(cont.)*

Peaceful Construction

Simulation

This simulation provides a way of practicing the skills learned in the Broken Squares. The purpose of this exercise is to experience the planning and carrying out of a cooperative effort and to teach us to appreciate and develop communication skills — both verbal and non-verbal — needed to work together for a common goal.

Using only toothpicks and popped popcorn, each pair of students will construct a structure. Then, they will find another pair and hook their construction to the other construction. And so on, until all constructions have been linked.

Group Instructions

Divide students into groups of 4-5. Give each set an equal amount of toothpicks and popped popcorn. Then read the following to the students.

> The purpose of this activity is to give us practice in cooperation as a way of setting, planning for, and reaching a goal, and to help us develop communication skills needed to succeed. Without communication, things have a way of not getting done. But there are many forms of communication. The most obvious form is speaking, but there are others we can and do also use.
>
> This is a cooperative building project. The toothpicks and popcorn are the building materials. Each group will have ten minutes to discuss the project, decide what to build, then plan how to build it.
>
> During this 10-minute planning time, you may plan and discuss all you want, but you may not touch the popcorn and toothpicks.
>
> At the end of the 10 minutes, I will give a signal.
>
> You may then begin to build; from then on, you may not talk. Only signaling will be allowed.
>
> At this point, check for understanding. Review procedure.
>
> The teacher may be the observer, or may choose one observer per group.
>
> Call the beginning of the ten-minute planning session. Teacher circulates. Observers stay with their group.
>
> Give signal. Say "Stop talking; begin building."
>
> When all groups have finished, discuss what happened.

Peace Journal Activities *(cont.)*

Peaceful Construction (cont.)

For Discussion

Discuss the problems encountered in linking the constructions. How were the problems resolved? If they were unable to resolve them, what did they do?

Look at the linked structures. Can you find your own? What happens when you linked yours with another? What was your construction in your pair? Is it still that now? Why not?

Interdependence means to rely on each other for support. In the directions for the construction, you were asked to depend upon each other and another pair for the support of your structure.

What are some positive things you learned from this exercise in interdependence?

Follow-Up Questions

Ask these questions after your discussion. Have children answer them or use them as writing topics for their Peace Journals.

- How did you feel about it?

- Did all the people in your group join in? Why or why not?

- Did one person become the leader? How did that make the others feel?

- Did anyone feel frustrated? Why?

- What happened that helped you work together better?

- Did you follow your plan? Why or why not?

- Did you learn something about cooperation? What?

- How was this simulation different from Broken Squares?

- How was this simulation similar to Broken Squares?

- What rules could you add to make it harder?

- What rules would make it easier?

Sending Letters for Peace

Write letters to people in authority or a group to tell them your ideas of how to achieve world peace. Write a clear purpose for your letter in the opening sentence. Thank the person for his/her attention. Request that he/she write back soon in response.

Include a return address. Decorate with symbols and pictures that mean peace to you. Remember to keep copies of the letters sent. The copies can be made into a peace action class book.

Here are organizations that can give you more information about peace and about how you can be a peacemaker. The addresses may be photocopied and used as labels.

Beyond War
Dept. P
222 High Street
Palo Alto, CA 94301

Children's Creative Response to Conflict
c/o Fellowship of Reconciliation
Dept. P, Box 271
Nyack, NY 10960

Friendship Force
Dept. P
South Tower One
CNN Center, Suite 575
Atlanta, GA 30303

National Peace Institute Foundation
Dept. P
110 Maryland Avenue, N.E.
Washington, D.C. 20002

Peacemakers, Inc.
Dept. P
P.O. Box 141254
Dallas, TX 75214

20/20 Vision
Dept. P
1819 High St., N.W.
Suite 1000
Washington, D.C. 20006

Idea List for Writing Letters Urging World Peace

Here are some ideas for places to write:

The President of the United States
1600 Pennsylvania Avenue
Washington, D.C. 20500

Humanitas International Humanrights Committee (HIHRC)
P.O. Box 818
Menlo Park, CA 94026

The American Friends Service Committee
Alternatives to Violence Project
3049 East Genesee Street
Syracuse, NY 13224

Don't forget senators, congresspeople, ambassadors, and visiting foreign dignitaries.

Center for International Policy on Human Rights
236 Massachusetts Ave., N.E.
Suite 505
Washington, D.C. 20002

Center for the Study of Human Rights
704 International Affairs Building
Columbia University
New York, NY 10027

American Alliance Against Violence
310 Fourth Ave.
Suite 612
Minneapolis, MN 55415

Amnesty International of the U.S.A.
322 Eighth Avenue
New York, N.Y. 10001

The United Nations

Office for Special Political Affairs
Observer Mission and Peacekeeping Forces
Room S-3853A
New York, NY 10017

Human Rights Committee
United Nations Center for Human Rights
Palais Des Nation
C.H.-1211
Geneva 10
Switzerland

UNICEF
3 United Nations Plaza
New York, NY 10017

Peace Wheel

Native Americans have long held a deep respect for peace and harmony. Read "Law of the Great Peace" found in *The Big Book for Peace*. Then read *Peace Begins with You*, this time looking for the steps involved in the peace process.

Use the steps involved in both readings to create sentences about the steps to peace. Write a sentence on each section. Then decorate your wheel with symbols of what peace means to you. Cut it out and glue it onto a piece of construction paper.

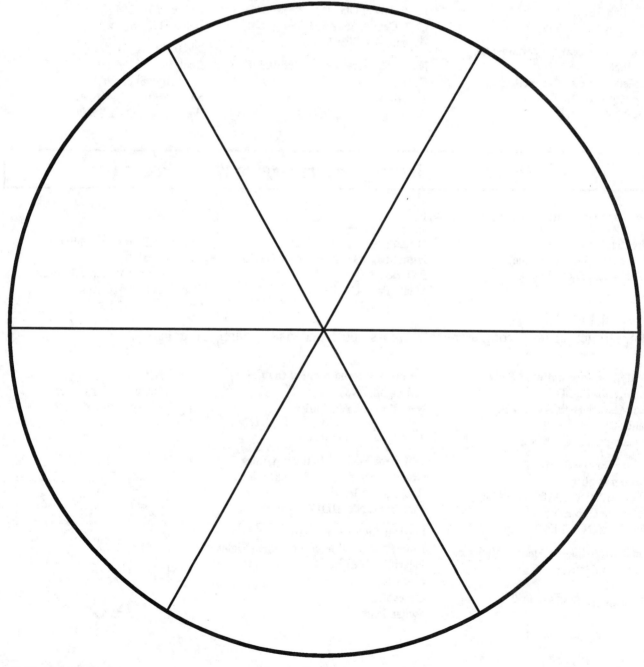

Peace in the News

Begin a collection of newspapers and magazines in your classroom.

Look through them first as a group. Find any articles on peace and cut them out. Include the date and source. Mount them on a wall chart.

Then, as a group, search for war articles (military intervention, military take-overs, etc.). Cut them out. Include the date and the source. Mount on the wall chart.

Your wall chart will look like this before you begin:

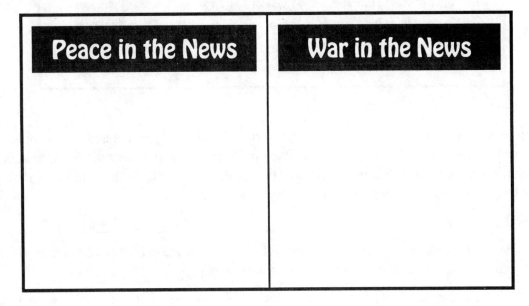

Peace in the News	War in the News

Discuss what was discovered. Why are there more articles on war than on peace? Note reasons at the bottom of the wall chart.

Keep your eyes open when reading newspapers at home. Bring in articles on peace or on war throughout the following week.

Add them to the wall chart daily. At the end of week one, what are your thoughts about the news. Continue this for the month.

Each week, complete the table and the open-ended sentences beneath the table. Respond to the open-ended questions each week. This will stretch you beyond the "easy" to the more thoughtful answers.

Have a group discussion when finished.

Playground Conflicts . . . Peaceful Solutions

Peaceful Solutions Chart

Approximate time involved in each step:

A. Define problem . . . . 5 minutes
B. Repeat problem aloud . . . . 2 minutes
C. Describe feelings . . . . 6 minutes
D. Discuss alternatives . . . . 5 minutes
E. Check for understanding . . . . 3 minutes
F. Agree to choose one alternative behavior . . . . 2 minutes
G. Choose alternative . . . . 6 minutes
H. Agree . . . . 2 minutes
I. Say, "Problem solved" . . . . 2 minutes

Conflict

Dominic and Sara are playing four square on the playground. Suddenly, Mike and Josh decide they want to play four square without Dominic and Sara. They push Dominic and Sara off the four square court, pushing Dominic to the ground. Dominic is angry at this treatment and hits both Mike and Josh in the nose. Mike's nose begins to bleed, and Josh falls and bumps his head.

A. What is the problem? _____

B. Use the Peaceful Solutions Chart to work through the steps of the problem. Do this as a role play among four students with the rest of the class as observers.

C. When the alternatives are named, have one of the people involved in the role play write them on the board. Ask if any observers have any additional alternatives to add. Then, proceed with the role play.

D. Keep track of the time involved in each part of the problem-solving steps. (Have someone not in the role play act as timekeeper.)

List the differences and similarities in each step below:

Actual time involved in each step	Peaceful Solutions Chart Time	Minutes Difference
A. _____	_____	_____
B. _____	_____	_____
C. _____	_____	_____
D. _____	_____	_____
E. _____	_____	_____
F. _____	_____	_____
G. _____	_____	_____
H. _____	_____	_____
I. _____	_____	_____

Playground Conflicts . . .
Peaceful Solutions *(cont.)*

In this activity you will tell time to the nearest five minutes and one minute.

First, draw in the time to the nearest five minutes. Label the time in the blank provided. Then, draw in the hands to the nearest minute. Label the time in the blank provided.

CLOCK #1 **CLOCK #2**

1. If Harry and William took 20 minutes to settle a conflict between them and they began their peaceful solution-making at 9:15 A.M., what time would it be when they finished?

   _____

2. Jim and Juanita had a conflict at the writing center. They began their peaceful solution-making at 2:15 P.M. It took them 33 minutes. What time was it when they were finished?

   _____

3. An argument took place in the class line. A discussion was held about it, and how it was against the rules. The discussion began at 11:24 A.M. It lasted until 12:07 P.M. How many minutes did it last? For this problem, show clock #1 when the discussion began and clock #2 for when it ended. Write the answer to how many minutes it took here.

   _____

4. Theresa, Jamie, and Vicki had a conflict in the lunchroom. Their three-way peaceful solution-making began at 10:24 A.M. It lasted until 11:37 A.M. How many minutes did their solution take? (Follow the same directions as #3)

   _____

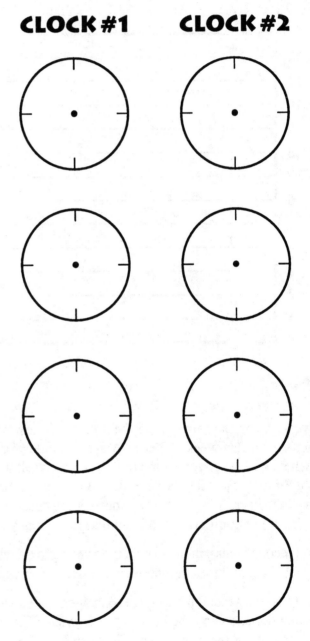

Challenge! On the back of this paper, write three problems of your own. Include your own name and other classmates' names in your problems.

How Am I Doing?

Teacher Note: Using the bar graphs provided, encourage your students to chart the number of conflicts they are engaged in throughout the week.

Begin by brainstorming what a conflict is. Develop a working list of ideas that encompass the class idea of conflict. Help the class by providing certain times immediately following time blocks to do their graphing. Do not let it wait until the end of the day.

Collect at the end of the week.

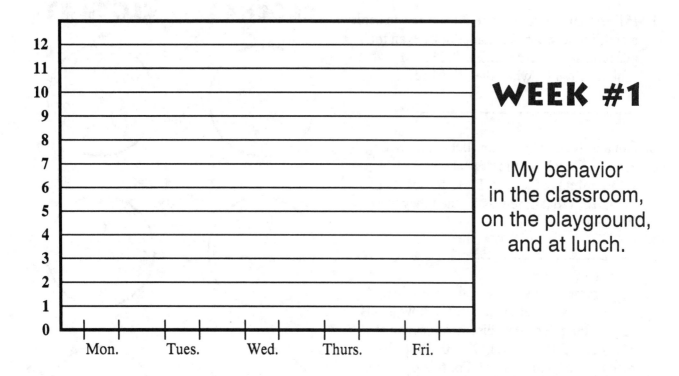

WEEK #1

My behavior
in the classroom,
on the playground,
and at lunch.

Give students the same graph sheet on the following Monday. Ask them if they see anything they can improve for this week. (Ideas: "Maybe I could work on not being so easily teased. I fly off the handle whenever I hear anyone tease me. I make myself a fun target that way." Or, "I think that I will not play with Emily for awhile. We are still having some problems after school. I want to work them out first." Or "I want to keep doing what I have been doing because it works just fine for me. I am not involved in outside or classroom conflicts. I work out disagreements as soon as they come up.")

This second week graph is very empowering to the class. It helps them to see immediately the importance of their own attitudes in their own behavior. Discuss learnings that have occurred to students.

Note that the second bar graph has an open-ended label. In this way, you could simply fold the top of the page under and copy the bottom graph twice. This way, you will be ready to have an open-ended set of two graphs on the same page. This can be done at other times throughout the year to help students to monitor their own behavior. Discuss after each week.

How Am I Doing?

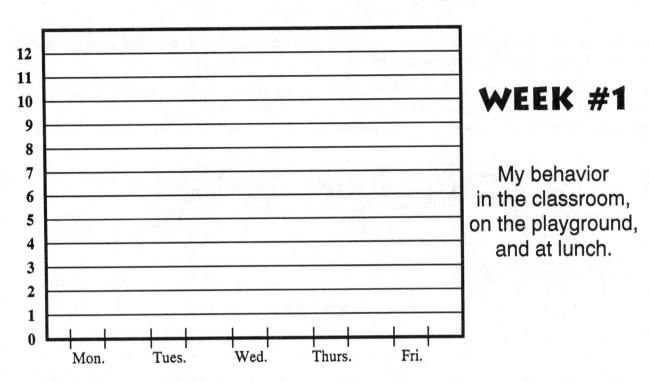

WEEK #1

My behavior
in the classroom,
on the playground,
and at lunch.

Begin with the top chart. Graph your behavior daily. Use your class chart on conflicts to see how many you had throughout the day. Think: How could you improve? What could you do to lower the number of conflicts in your own daily life?

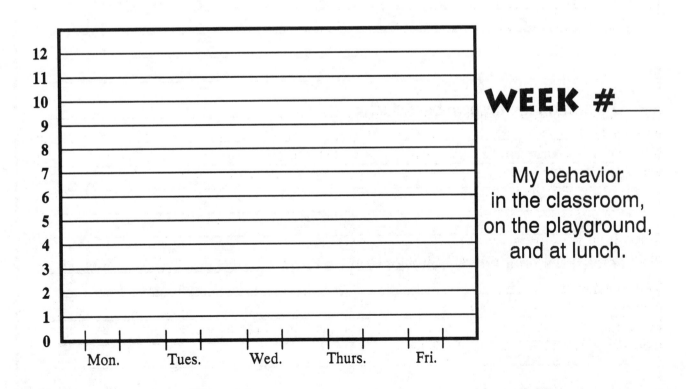

WEEK #___

My behavior
in the classroom,
on the playground,
and at lunch.

Personal AHAS!

Create an "AHA!" area in your room where you can display the "AHA" pages of understanding. Sometimes our own discoveries about our behavior surprise us!

After you have completed two weeks of bar graphing your behavior (page 51) and comparing the two graphs, reproduce the chart below for each child to list his or her own personal "AHAS!"

My Personal "AHAS!"

I learned that _____
_____
_____
_____
_____
_____

I was surprised to find out _____
_____
_____
_____
_____
_____

I have changed my own behavior by _____
_____
_____
_____
_____

I have **not** changed my behavior in these ways _____
_____
_____
_____
_____
_____

Peace in Any Language

Peace on Earth

Below are ways to say "May Peace Prevail on Earth" in many languages! Can you find additional languages?

◆ • ◆ • ◆ • ◆ • ◆ • ◆ • ◆ • ◆ • ◆ • ◆

Arabic   السلام للعالم أجمع

Chinese   我們祈祷世界人類的和平

French   *Puisse la Paix régner dans le monde*

German   *Möge Fried auf Erden sein*

Greek   *Εὔχομαι να επικρατήσει η ειρήνη στον κόσμο*

Hebrew   ישרה שלום עלי אדמות

Gaelic   *Go mBeidh Siothchain Go Deo Ar Thalamh An Domhain*

Italian   *Che la pace possa regnare sulla terra*

Navaho   *Nahasdzáán Bikáági Táá axtsogóó hozhóo dooleex*

Philipino   *Sanáy Manatili Ang Kapayapaan Sa Mundo*

Polish   *Niech ludzkosc swiata zyje w pokooju*

Russian   Да будет мир человечеству во всем мире

Spanish   *Que La Paz Prevalezca En La Tierra*

Swahili   *Amani Iwe ul mwenguni*

_____

_____

_____

_____

World

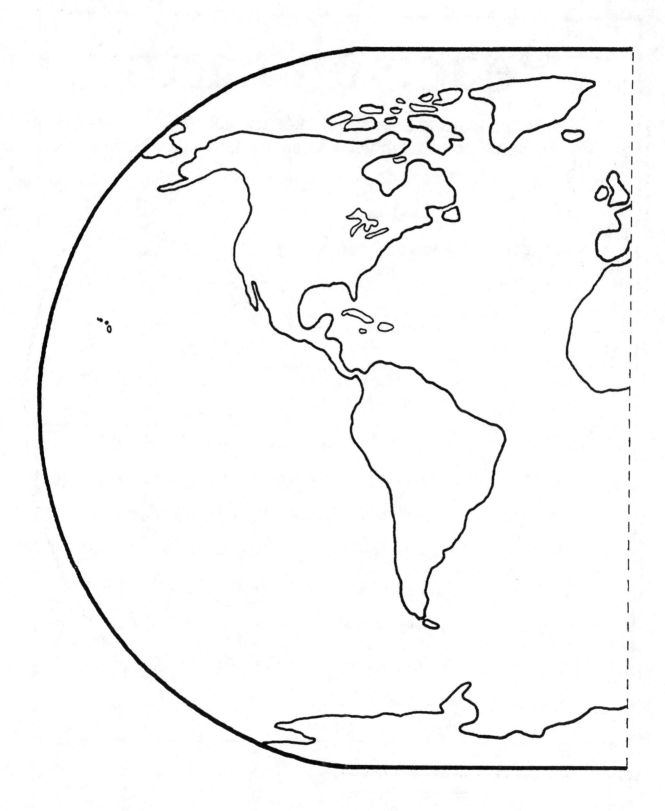

Map

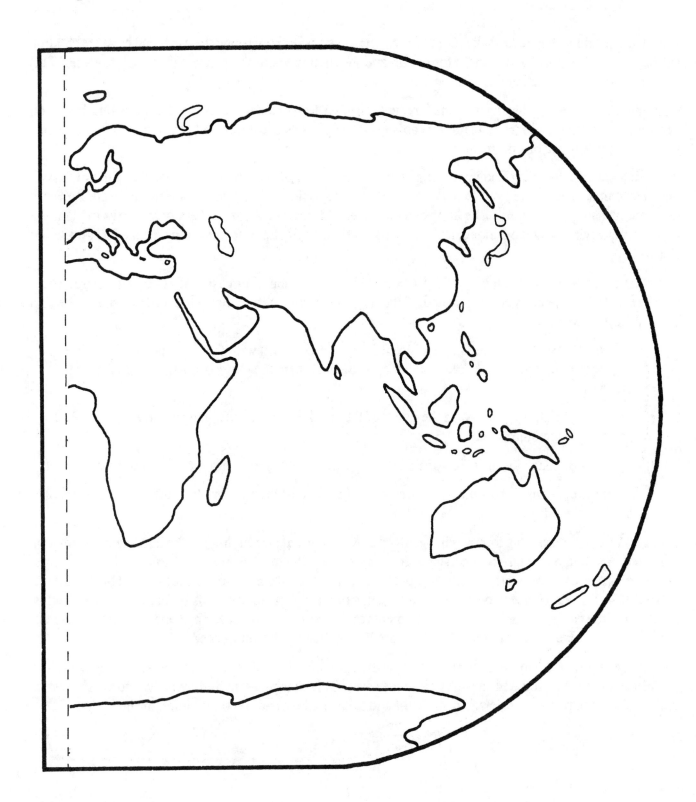

Directions:

1. Locate the countries whose languages are included in the phrases, "Peace on Earth."

2. Locate the countries currently at conflict. Mark them with red dots.

Peacemaker Cards

Have students make the Peacemaker Cards found on pages 57-59. Reproduce the cards and have the children cut them out. Have them glue the information and the picture about the peacemaker back-to-back. This will begin their Peacemaker Card collection.

Continue the project by having students create their own Peacemaker Cards. After collecting books on peacemakers from the library, students can do research in pairs. Have them use encyclopedias, newspapers, and any other sources of information.

As students work, they may find interesting symbols, phrases, poems, songs, or quotes that will not fit with their particular peacemaker, but that would fit the peace topic. To accommodate these, begin a "Peace Collection" spot where other peace ideas can be placed. If you take a moment every few days to highlight these by simply reading them aloud, students will continue to dig up other additional peace ideas and your file will grow!

Use the Peacemaker Cards on pages 57-59 as models. Let students suggest that other peace cards could also be created by the class and duplicated. Other topics for cards within the peace framework include (but are not limited to):

- the word "peace" in other languages (one language per card) with the word peace in English and the other language on one side, and a map showing where the other language is spoken on the other side.

- quotes highlighting peace with the name of the speaker on one side, and the time and place (if known) on the other side.

- symbols of peace identified on one side; where the symbols are found, or used on the other side.

- symbols created by the students on one side; the name of the creator and a bit about the symbol on the other side.

Being concise is an art. This format will "gently force" that art! It also highlights the important information collected, and demonstrates an understanding of the topic. The teacher may need to model several times how to make cards step-by-step to alleviate potential confusion. Comparison to football and baseball cards is helpful — it is also helpful to suggest that students bring in their sports cards before this project begins. Analysis of the cards can yield a list of the elements of the card. Then a list can be generated of the elements that the peacemaker cards will include. Post that list on the wall for reference.

It is suggested that the teacher purchase the plastic sports card holders (they are most economical when purchased in packs of 100). Each page holds nine cards. This finishing touch adds so much to the enjoyment and appreciation of the cards created, and will add to the enthusiasm of continuation of the project.

Peacemaker Cards

Mohandas Karamchand Gandhi

(1869-1948) India

In 1915, Gandhi led the Indian nationalist movement and used peace to help free Britain. India considers Gandhi the father of its nation.

Jane Addams

(1860-1935)
United States

In 1889, Jane Addams and Ellen Gates Starr founded Chicago's Hull House where they set up the first public playground, and the first kindergarten. In 1931, Jane Addams was awarded the Nobel Peace Prize for her work with the Women's International League for Peace and Freedom.

Albert Schweitzer

(1875-1965) Germany

In 1902, Albert Schweitzer became a medical missionary. Over the years, he built a large hospital and medical station in Africa where he treated thousands of Africans every year. In 1952, Albert Schweitzer won the Nobel Peace Prize.

Martin Luther King Jr.

(1929-1968)
United States

Martin Luther King Jr., a Baptist minister, was against segregated seating on public buses. King did not believe in violence; he used only peaceful methods of protest. In 1963, he led the historic march on Washington and delivered his famous "I have a dream" speech. A year later, Martin Luther King Jr. was awarded the Nobel Peace Prize for leading nonviolent civil rights demonstrations.

Peacemaker Cards *(cont.)*

Nelson Mandela

(1918-) South Africa

Nelson Mandela was put into prison in 1962 for protesting how black people were being treated in South Africa. He began his protests in the 1950's because blacks were not allowed to vote and they were separated from whites by a policy called apartheid.
In 1992, Mandela was released from prison and continued to work for his cause, equality for black people.

Dag Hammarskjold

(1905-1961) Sweden

Dag Hammarskjold was Secretary-General of the United Nations from 1953-1961. He helped solve the problems between the United States and the Soviet Union, and the Suez crisis between Egypt and Israel and Israel's allies, France and Great Britain. After his death, Hammarskjold was awarded the 1961 Nobel Peace Prize for his efforts to bring peace to the Congo.

Mother Teresa

(1910-) Macedonia

Mother Teresa's real name was Agnes Gonxha Bojaxhiu. In 1928, she joined a religious order which sent her to India to work with the poor and needy. In 1979 she received the Nobel Peace prize for her work with the poor.

Theodore Roosevelt

(1858-1919)
United States

As president of the United States in 1905, Theodore Roosevelt helped end the Russo-Japanese War. He did this by bringing representatives from both Russia and Japan together for peace talks. These talks led to the Treaty of Portsmouth. Because of his work, he became the first American to win the Nobel Peace Prize.

58

Peacemaker Cards *(cont.)*

William Penn

(1644-1718) London

Penn believed in religious freedom and the right of individuals to worship as they pleased. He wanted to settle a land where people were free to worship in their own way without fear. With the permission of King Charles II, William Penn founded what is known as the state of Pennsylvania. The name Pennsylvania means ''Penn's Woods.''

Chief Seattle

United States

Chief Seattle was a respected and peaceful leader of one of the Northwest Nations. In the mid 1850's Chief Seattle delivered a speech in his native tongue while in Washington, D.C., prior to the signing of a paper where the United States would buy the Indian's Territory. In part, he said, ''The earth does not belong to us. We belong to the earth. If we sell you our land, care for it as we have cared for it. Preserve the land and the air and the rivers for your children's children and love it as we have loved it.''

Red Cross

The Red Cross works to relieve human suffering. More than 135 nations have Red Cross societies. Each Red Cross worker tries to prevent suffering in time of war or peace, and serves all peoples regardless of race, nationality, or religion.
The name ''Red Cross'' comes from the organization's flag, a red cross on a white background.

Peacemaker Research

Research and find out more about famous peacemakers and how each helped to further the cause of peace. You may choose one from the list or choose one of your own. Use the form on page 61 to write a report.

Important information to include is name, date of birth, country worked in, peacemaking activities, and quotes. Draw a picture or, if included, use the pictures from the Peacemaker Cards.

- Abraham Johannes Muste
- Albert Luthuli
- Albert Schweitzer
- Archbishop Desmond Tutu
- Carmen Delgado Votaw
- Cesar Chavez
- Dag Hammarskjold
- George Fox
- George C. Marshall
- Jane Addams
- Jeannette Rankin
- Mahatma Gandhi
- Martin Luther King
- Mother Teresa
- Nelson Mandela
- Norman Thomas
- Rosa Parks
- Sarah Winemucca
- Shirley Chisholm
- Teddy Roosevelt
- William Penn
- Woodrow Wilson

Peacemaker Research Report Form

Name _____   Date _____

Peacemaker REPORT

My report is about

_____

This peacemaker was/is from

_____

Picture of Peacemaker

This person is known as a peacemaker because

_____

_____

_____

_____

_____

_____

_____

Nobel Prize Winners

The Nobel Prize is an award given every year for someone who has made a major contribution to peace in the world. The winner gets both a medal and money. The money comes from the estate of Alfred Nobel, who invented dynamite. Mr. Nobel was disappointed that his invention was not used for peaceful purposes. So before he died in 1896 he set up the Nobel Foundation. This organization makes awards each year to someone who has contributed to the "good of humanity."

Find the names of the Nobel Peace Prize winners in the puzzle below.

Albert Schweitzer	Lech Walesa	Willy Brandt
Mother Teresa	Jane Addams	Menachem Begin
Anwar el-Sadat	Mikhail Gorbachev	

```
M E O Q L J U I P O C W G I O S
G U E O Z C I N W I E I U L D N
I H Y S G L E C H W A L E S A O
W A A I E H N H E H V L O L T A
S F L X M Q R R A M E Y D L A M
N I B H N A E G N L T B E S E O
E D E T A U M H W E O R D T R T
S M R E P E E S A O G A A O I H
T J T A X D N O R V Z N L L S E
K I S C D J A N E A D D A M S R
D E C E I L C W L A S T A A F T
A M H H Y T H Q S O U O A N O E
M R W O S A E T A T M D V B D R
S F E S H W M R D L S E S F T E
I H I L M H B P A N T L E O O S
E L T I A P E V T I R D E B R A
M S Z M E O G E E C I Y M U S A
A E E L B W I I D O F T E T I E
I P R V C L N W S I R H F C T A
M I K H A I L G O R B A C H E V
```

Symbols of Peace Mobile

Directions: Reproduce the symbols on pages 63-64. A blank is provided for children to make their own. Have children color them and cut them out. Punch holes at the top of each circle, add yarn and tie them onto a hanger. Hang the mobiles up.

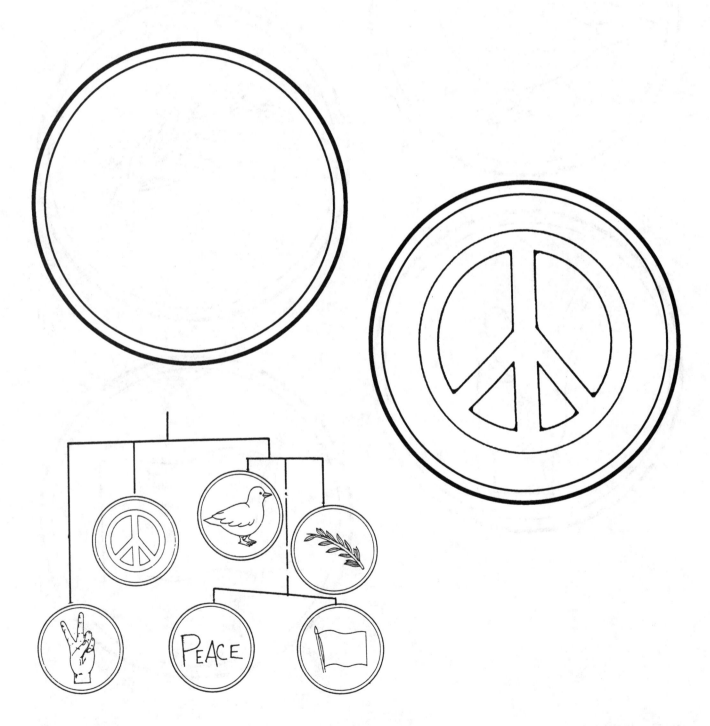

Symbols of Peace Mobile *(cont.)*

64

Mandala Designs

Mandala designs are designs in a circular pattern. Mandalas emphasize the harmony of the circle and are used by Native Americans to remind us of the harmony in living in peace with nature. Children will need an 8" (20 cm) square piece of plain paper and crayons.

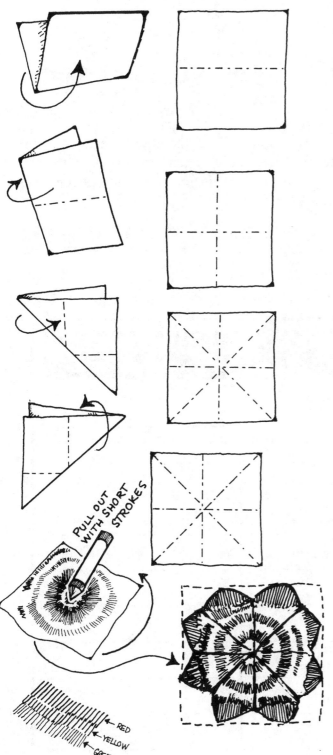

- Fold edge to edge. Crease. Open.

- Repeat with other edge. Open.

- Fold corner to corner. Crease. Open.

- Repeat with other edge. Crease. Open.

- You now have eight folds.

- Begin in the very center with your crayon.

- Push hard.

- Pull out from the center with your crayon, turning the paper as you do.

- Next, choose a new color. Pull out from the edge of the last color. Turn the paper.

- You will see a colorburst begin to appear.

- Continue for 5-7 more colors.

- Then, use the creases to form small petals.

- Next, outline in black.

Group Soup

Make some peace group soup to share with each other. This is a fun class project as students begin to see the payoff in cooperating.

Directions: Divide the class into three groups.

- Group 1 will provide the vegetables for the soup.

- Group 2 will provide the meat for the soup.

- Group 3 will provide the paper bowls, soup spoons, and napkins.

The teacher needs to provide a crockpot and a ladle.

Discuss the making of a group soup. Include in your discussion facts about the need for many different ingredients for the soup to be very tasty. Then discuss the concept of when many people work together less is needed from each person. So, if someone said he or she could bring in tomatoes, only one is needed, and so on.

Divide a large piece of paper into thirds. Have the students complete the chart as shown below with their name and what they will provide. The next day, bring a crockpot to school. Peel and chop the ingredients together as a class. Cook all day. Serve and eat.

Note: Each class soup will be different. Most times it will be more a stew than a soup!

GROUP #1 Vegetables	GROUP #2 Meat	GROUP #3 Bowls, spoon, bread

66

Peace Snack

Cooperation makes any job easier! Fill out the chart below to see who will bring what. Combine the ingredients for a healthy, munchable snack! Remember to check to be sure no one in the class is allergic to or dietarily prohibited from any ingredients.

POPPED POPCORN	APPLES	NUTS	CEREAL
_____	_____	_____	_____
_____	_____	_____	_____
_____	_____	_____	_____
_____	_____	_____	_____
_____	_____	_____	_____
_____	_____	_____	_____
_____	_____	_____	_____
_____	_____	_____	_____
_____	_____	_____	_____
_____	_____	_____	_____

Enjoy your Peace Snack!
It was made with your help and the help of your classmates.
Enjoy the peace you share now!

Peace Pole

Peace is a focus you may want to maintain throughout the academic year! One way to maintain that focus is to erect a peace pole as a constant reminder of the goal of peace. Several steps need to be considered.

The first is getting funding for your project. An idea that could be tried would be to collect money from students. The money collected could then be matched by the parents or a parent organization.

- A fun fair could be held with the profits to be donated for a Peace Pole. (See pages 28-29 for some ideas for a peace fair that could be adapted for a school-wide fair.)

- An in-house grant could be written to secure sponsorship of a Peace Pole.

The class could write letters to the principal stating their preference.

Next, education needs to be done. Informing parents of the meaning and impact of peace-pole sponsorship will make the process less mysterious. Also, it will help to alleviate any fears that may arise. Invite parents to the dedication ceremony.

While these two parts are being done, it would be helpful to obtain the information packets from both the addresses below:

The Peace Pole Makers, U.S.A.
3534 Lanham Road
Maple City, MI 49664
Telephone: (616) 334-4567

The Peace Pole Project
3239 Sacramento Street
San Francisco, CA 94115
Telephone: (415) 563-0708

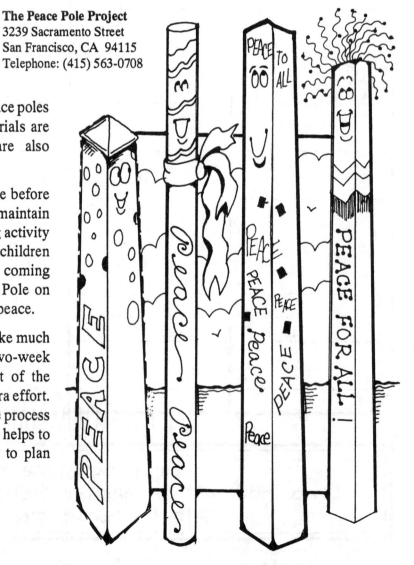

These are the actual makers of all of the peace poles for the North American continent. Materials are available upon request. Price lists are also available.

Decide upon the reasons for the peace pole before requesting funding and you will be able to maintain your focus. Paramount to this culminating activity is parents demonstrating a belief in their children as peaceful leaders of tomorrow through coming together to plant and dedicate the Peace Pole on school grounds as a constant reminder of peace.

This particular culminating activity will take much planning, and may go beyond the week to two-week unit plan. However, the overall benefit of the activity will be well worth the time and extra effort. Involving the students in every facet of the process will yield the most benefit to them. It also helps to teach participatory government and how to plan and execute the plans.

　　　　68

Peace-Pole Book Marks

This is one idea used to give the students something tangible to take home after the dedication of the Peace Pole. Have them create their own in the blank.

Classroom Peace Quilt

A wonderful addition to any classroom is a "peace quilt." This allows students to express their individual feelings about peace, and then to have them joined with others in their classroom. This can be done using materials or construction paper.

Materials: muslin or calico
backing material
yarn
thread
needle
puffy paint
fabric crayons
permanent markers
pattern, page 71

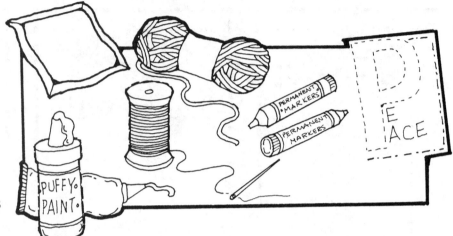

Directions: Cut out muslin squares according to the pattern on page 71. Make the inner square and tell each student only to draw in the inner square. The drawing should reflect what peace means to each individual student. It can be puffy-painted, fabric-crayoned or permanent-markered. You may ask parents to do the sewing or have children use a large needle and thread and stitch together only the border.

Note: The whole project can be done with construction paper, glue, crayons, and scissors.

Peace Quilt Pattern

Bulletin Board

Objective

This bulletin board will be used to emphasize the smallness of the world, the interdependence of us all, and the beauty of languages.

Materials: green and white butcher paper   crayons

scissors   colorful map pins

stapler

Construction

Staple a green background to a bulletin board.

Cut out dove pattern (page 74), stuff with recycled paper and set aside.

Place world pattern (page 75) in opaque projector, trace, and cut. Have students color the land green and the oceans blue. Cut out a blue circle of the same size, staple to the back of the world and stuff with recycled paper.

Cut letters from white paper or use the letters on page 73.

Have each student bring in a recent photo and overlap them.

Add the word "peace" in different languages. (See page 76.)

Directions:

Add the word peace and the separate language label daily. Say peace in that language together. Each day, as a new language is added, repeat the previous day's word. At week's end, repeat all five languages. After eight days, remove the language labels and ask students which is which.

After ten days, have students pin the location of the languages they have on the map on the bulletin board.

PEACE THROUGHOUT THE WORLD

Bulletin Board *(cont.)*

Bulletin Board *(cont.)*

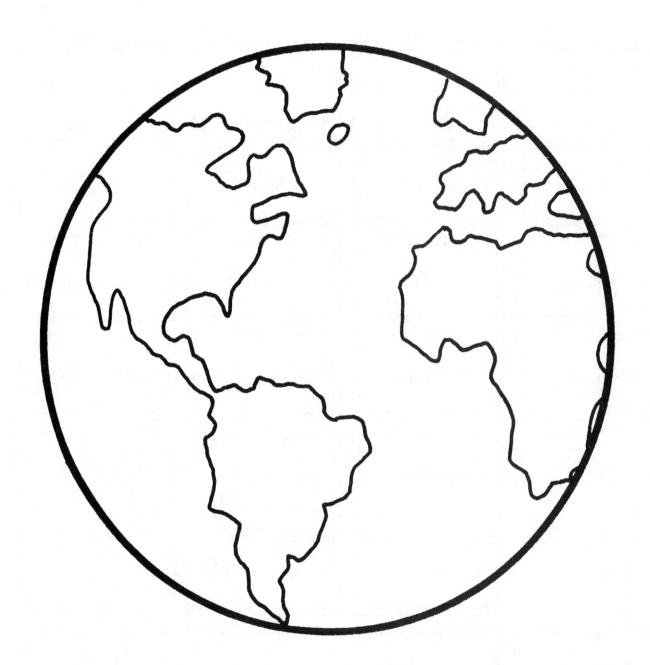

Bulletin Board (cont.)

Peace in Many Languages

Arabic	sah-LAAM	Irish	SHEE-ah-kahn
Chinese	hoh ping	Italian	PAH-cheh
French	pay	Navaho	hoh-zho
German	FREE-deh	Polish	spoh-KOY
Greek	eh-REE-nee	Russian	meer
Hawaiian	mah-loo-HEE-ah	Spanish	pahth
Hebrew	sha-LOHM	Swahili	ah-MAHN-ee

76

Peace Certificate

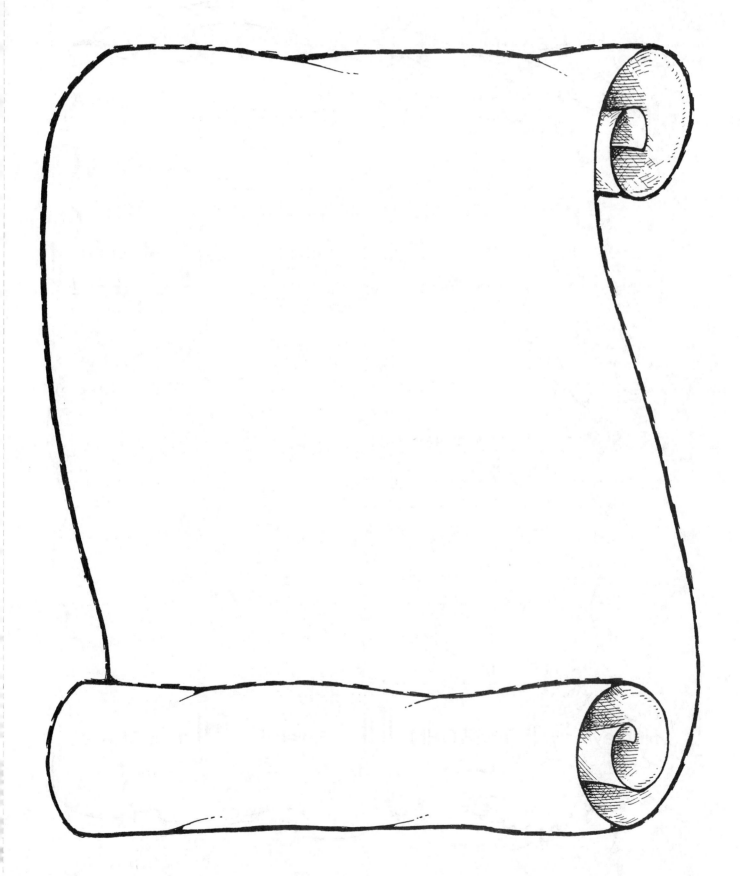

Peaceful Stationery

Bibliography

Audiotapes

Grammer, Red. *Teaching Peace*. Smilin' Atcha Music, 1986.

Krehbiel, Jude and Doug. *I Can Make Peace*. MCC, 1983.

Videotapes

Children's Art Exchange. Children's Art Exchange, 1985.

Fighting Fair: Dr. Martin Luther King, Jr. for Kids. Grace C. Abrams Peace Education Foundation, 1986.

Sadako and the Thousand Paper Cranes. Informed Democracy, 1990.

Fiction

Aardema, Verna. *Rabbit Makes a Monkey of Lion*. Dial, 1989.

Ashbrenner, Brent, and Melissa. *Gavriel and Jemal: Two Boys of Jerusalem*. Dodd, Mead & Co., 1984.

Bishop, Claire Huchet. *Twenty and Ten, 1952*. Peter Smith, 1984.

Coerr, Eleanor. *Sadako and the Thousand Paper Cranes*. Dell, 1977.

Heide, Florence Parry and Judith Heide Gilliland. *Sami and the Time of the Troubles*. Clarion, 1992.

Hoffman, Hoffman. *Amazing Grace*. Dial, 1991.

Hutton, Warwick. *The Trojan Horse*. McElderry/Macmillan, 1992.

Innocenti, Roberto. *Rose Blanche*. Stewart, Tabori & Chang, 1991.

Isadora, Rachel. *At the Crossroads*. Greenwillow, 1991.

Lattimore, Deborah. *The Flame of Peace: A Tale of the Aztecs*. Harper Trophy, 1987.

Lewis, C.S. *The Chronicles of Narnia*. Collier, 1970.

Maruki, Toshi. *Hiroshima No Pika*. Lothrop, 1980.

Ringold, Faith. *Aunt Harriet's Underground Railroad in the Sky*. Crown, 1992.

Shemin, Margaretha. *The Little Riders*. Putnam, 1963.

White Deer of Autumn. *Ceremony in the Circle of Life*. Beyond Words Publishing, 1983.

Teacher Resources

Alternatives to Violence Project Manual. Alternatives to Violence Program, 3049 East Genesee Street, Syracuse, NY 13224.

Barnaby, Frank. *The Gaia Peace Atlas: Survival into the Third Millennium*. Doubleday, 1988.

Beck, Sanderson. *The Way to Peace: The Great Peacemakers, Philosophers of Peace and Efforts Toward World Peace*. Coleman, Farmingdale, 1986.

Judson, Stephanie, ed. *A Manual On Nonviolence and Children*. New Society Publishers, 1984.

Broken Squares are used by permission of Steve Angell. The manual is not copyrighted.

Interhelp
P.O. 331
Northampton, MA 01061

Peace Organizations

Peace Development Fund
44 North Prospect Street
P.O. 270
Amherst, MA 01004.

United States Institute of Peace
1550 M Street, N.W.
Suite 700
Washington, D.C. 20005-1708

Teacher Note: Following are two sources that may be of interest in your research. *Pacifist: Adventures in Courage*, M.V. Fox and the National Women's History Project in Windsor, CA (707) 838-6000.

Answer Key

Note: Many activities in this book do not have answers. This is because so much of the unit is based on thoughts and feelings in reaction to the readings that it does not make sense to include an answer key for them. Challenges can be made, however, for illogical or baseless answers. This unit provides an arena for expression, and an ability for using higher level thinking skills in a very real way.

Page 10

warm	bright
strong	calm
cool	gentle
busy	loud
different	quietest
complete	calmest
lonely	good
protected	loved
braver	afraid
stronger	study
pain	learn
year	have
danger	hope
lives	work
grows	want
spreads	

Page 62

```
M E O Q L J U I P O C W G I O S
G U E O Z C I N W I E I U L D N
I H Y S G L E C H W A L E S A O
W A A I E H N H E H V L O L T A
S F L X M Q R R A M E Y D L A M
N I B H N A E G N L T B E S E O
E D E T A U M H W E O R D T R T
S M R E P E E S A O G A A O I H
T J T A X D N O R V Z N L L S E
K I S C D J A N E A D D A M S R
D E C E I L C W L A S T A A F T
A M H H Y T H Q S O U O A N O E
M R W O S A E T A T M D V B D R
S F E S H W M R D L S E S F T E
I H I L M H B P A N T L E O O S
E L T I A P E V T I R D E B R A
M S Z M E O G E E C I Y M U S A
A E E L B W I I D O F T E T I E
I P R V C L N W S I R H F C T A
M I K H A I L G O R B A C H E V
```

Page 22

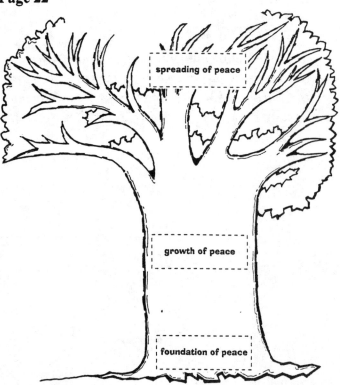

spreading of peace

growth of peace

foundation of peace